IMAGES
of America

ROCHESTER
NEIGHBORHOODS

"The Wings of Progress," a 1929 Art Deco structure, dominates the corner of Broad Street and Exchange at Rochester's Times Square. The building's unusual design has been interpreted as a representation of a bishop's mitre, knight's helmet, or bird wings, but the building's name reveals the intent of its designer. Canal boats once docked at Child's Basin on the canal, located on the west side of the river opposite the building. Here, the Erie Canal's boatloads of passengers and goods crossed the river on an arched aqueduct. The *Times-Union* newspaper was published at the Gannett Newspapers building on the corner to the south. This photograph was taken in 1956.

IMAGES
of America

ROCHESTER
NEIGHBORHOODS

Shirley Cox Husted and Ruth Rosenberg-Naparsteck

ARCADIA
PUBLISHING

Published by Arcadia Publishing
Charleston, South Carolina

Library of Congress Catalog Card Number: 00-104065

For all general information contact Arcadia Publishing at:
Telephone 843-853-2070
Fax 843-853-0044
E-mail sales@arcadiapublishing.com
For customer service and orders:
Toll-Free 1-888-313-2665

Visit us on the Internet at www.arcadiapublishing.com

To Dr. Blake McKelvey, Rochester city historian, 1948–1973, and those other friends of history whose interest and support has made our work possible: Mayor Thomas Ryan, Mayor William Johnson, Monroe County Manager Gordon Howe and Monroe County Executive Lucien Morin. Their service to the people has changed history forever.

Acknowledgments

Many of the fascinating photographs and pieces of memorabilia reproduced here are from the files of the Rochester Public Library's Local History Division, the City of Rochester Photo Lab, and the files of the city historian and the Parma town historian. Others came from the Honorable Gordon A. Howe, Mrs. Oscar Smith, and several other individuals. Special thanks to Ira Srole at the City of Rochester Photo Lab for developing images on glass plate negatives and for many other reproductions. We are grateful to Everett Farwell and the California Historical Society, Rick Hooper, Marion Schepler, Henry Gabelle, Carol Fede, Shirley Iverson, and the staff at Local History, Lloyd Klos and Gannett Newspapers, and Pam O'Neil, Amy Sutton, Peter Turco, and other staff members at Arcadia Publishing. Without their assistance, this book could not have been published.

Maps of Rochester's early neighborhoods were created by the City of Rochester Department of Community Development using a 1984 base map of major streets.

CONTENTS

Two young girls on the beach experience the joy of summertime in a beachfront neighborhood. (From the Mitchell Collection at the Parma Town Hall.)

FOREWORD

The history of our city is really the history of our neighborhoods, each having a unique character. They were established at different periods, and their character reflects that. Some neighborhoods began as pioneer settlements that were absorbed as the city grew. Many of our streets have a curious jog—a dog leg—that marks the boundary of an early settlement. One neighborhood has a bend in the road, a remnant of its history as a race track; another has a series of streets named for trees and flowers. Still others have houses intermingled with old mills and warehouses. Kids play baseball on empty lots, and vendors sell hot dogs on the sidewalk. In some neighborhoods, the names of businesses change every few decades, reflecting the changing ethnic character. Our neighborhoods are the life of our city. That is where people live their lives, raise their children, and create their idea of a community. While the history of our neighborhoods is ever changing, they still bear a close resemblance to those of earlier generations.

This book features some of the neighborhoods in our city's past. It is a sharing of snapshots at various times in our city's history—much as you would see in a family's scrapbook.

I hope this book launches a curiosity about your own neighborhood and gives you roots—a sense of where you have been and where you are. People tend to think of history as our past, but we are empowered when we realize that our actions shape our history—we form it ourselves. What great power we have to make our neighborhoods, our city, "the best place to live and raise a family."

—Ruth Rosenberg-Naparsteck
Rochester City Historian

INTRODUCTION

At one time, Rochester's neighborhoods were widely separated infant settlements. They were sometimes named for their agricultural heritage, such as the neighborhoods of Swillburg, Goat Hill, the Butter Bowl, and Bull's Head. They were also named for their residents' place of origin—Cork, Dublin, and Dutchtown—and some were named for European locales such as Frankfort, Carthage, and Athens. Some neighborhoods took the name of individuals: Charlotte, King's Landing, Hanford's Landing, Castletown, McCrackenville, Kelsey's Landing, Tryon Town, and Lincoln Park. The rich Ruffled Shirt District was named for its prominent patrician residents who wore immaculate ruffled shirts and lived in stately houses.

Today, these early neighborhoods are part of a great metropolis of more than 100 various neighborhoods, echoing that worthy American slogan, *E Pluribus Unum*, "From Many, One." Rochester, New York, is a neighborhood of neighborhoods, each of which has maintained its own identity. Charlotte, a village somewhat unwillingly annexed, still considers itself an individual locality. Charlotte became the port of the Genesee in 1805, and soon land sales there outstripped those at Kings's Landing, the 1798 settlement that later became the site of Eastman Kodak Company, a leading Rochester industry. Residents called the Kodak locality "the End of the Ridge" into the middle of the 19th century, remembering the time when Ridge Road ended at the riverbank. Construction of a bridge changed that isolation and made it possible for city residents and Irondequoit's citizens to find easily accessible employment at George Eastman's ever-growing industrial complex of laboratories and factories.

The milling industry that flourished along the central stretch of the Genesee River as it wound its quiet way through Rochester began with Ebenezer Allan's rude long mill, built in 1789 beside today's Broad Street. Successive millers who harnessed the power of the Genesee River called it "the Flour City." But by the middle of the 19th century, the seed industry and widespread production of flowers, trees, and shrubs began turning it into "the Flower City," supplying root stock, seeds, and bulbs across the world. Then came a career as "the Picture City," thanks to Eastman Kodak, while today's role as "the World's Image Centre" acknowledges the importance of the Xerox Corporation and Bausch & Lomb's optical products. Leadership in the info-technological and telecommunications field has brought a suggestion for a new title, "Telecom Alley." The area's 75 telecommunication companies now lead the state in payroll growth, but that growth represents only about one percent of the total Rochester payroll. Others feel that it should be recognized as a music center or an idea capital, the home of many inventions that forever changed society.

The infant village that became Rochesterville in 1817 lay mostly west of the river on the storied 100-acre tract that Nathaniel Rochester and his associates, Charles Carroll and William Fitzhugh, had acquired. This land lay in what was first the town of Gates, then, after 1822, part of the town of Greece, until it was incorporated as a village in 1834. Founded by those three southern gentlemen who once had owned slaves but later freed them, Rochester became a haven on the Underground Railroad between 1830 and 1860. From Kelsey's Landing and the wharves at Charlotte, sympathetic ship captains transported runaways to Canada. Since they were technically free the moment they stepped aboard a British ship, it was here at Rochester that 100 or more weary fugitives found freedom each year in those tumultuous times before the Civil War. Some citizens blamed the abolitionists for causing that war, while others praised them. Some angrily charged that the South had destroyed the Union. Out of the turmoil and controversy came new political parties, the Republican party, the Liberty party, and the Free Soil party. Following this were crusades for female suffrage and alcoholic temperance, movements in which Rochester's women, led by Susan Brownell Anthony, played great leadership roles.

Independent, sometimes outrageous, outspoken, colorful and courageous, many of Rochester's leaders lie now in peaceful cemeteries along the riverside at Rapids Cemetery, Hincher Cemetery in Charlotte, Riverside Cemetery, Holy Sepulchre, or Mount Hope Cemetery. Beautiful Mount Hope Cemetery, the nation's first municipal burial ground, is located on the pinnacle of the only mountain range in Monroe County. Through it runs a portion of the old Native American trail that once brought Seneca families along the river, exploring, hunting and enjoying the glories of the Genesee River Valley.

Along with patriots and civic leaders, Holy Sepulchre contains the grave of the extroverted Dr. Francis Tumblety, suspected as the notorious Jack the Ripper. John Littlechild, a Scotland Yard investigator, revealed to a friend that he felt Dr. Francis Tumulty (also known as Tumblety) was the most likely suspect in the murder investigation. Tumulty was an eccentric patent medicine manufacturer and traveling huckster whose weird costumes and flamboyant behavior—along with a ghoulish collection of pickled female body parts—inspired such grave suspicions that he was questioned. He was released for lack of sufficient evidence. After he left England, the murders ceased. Briefly, he was also suspected of conspiracy in the assassination of Pres. Abraham Lincoln. Now he rests in lot 73, section 13, at Holy Sepulchre. Saints and sinners, heroes and rascals, the well-known and the unknown souls buried and forgotten in Potter's Fields all rest in peace, while on the southern slope of Mount Hope blossoms one of the largest lilac gardens in the world.

The city has always been an ethnic haven, a hotbed for inventors and reformers, an educational and spiritual leader, and a locality whose great variety is seen in its multitude of diverse neighborhoods, each an important part of the city's tapestry. Each neighborhood is a thread into which yesterday, today, and tomorrow will always be woven. It is our hope that these antique photographs will help to illustrate that image of a growing city, blending many aspects to create "Rochester, Our Rochester!"

—Shirley Cox Husted

One

THE CITY BY THE FALLS

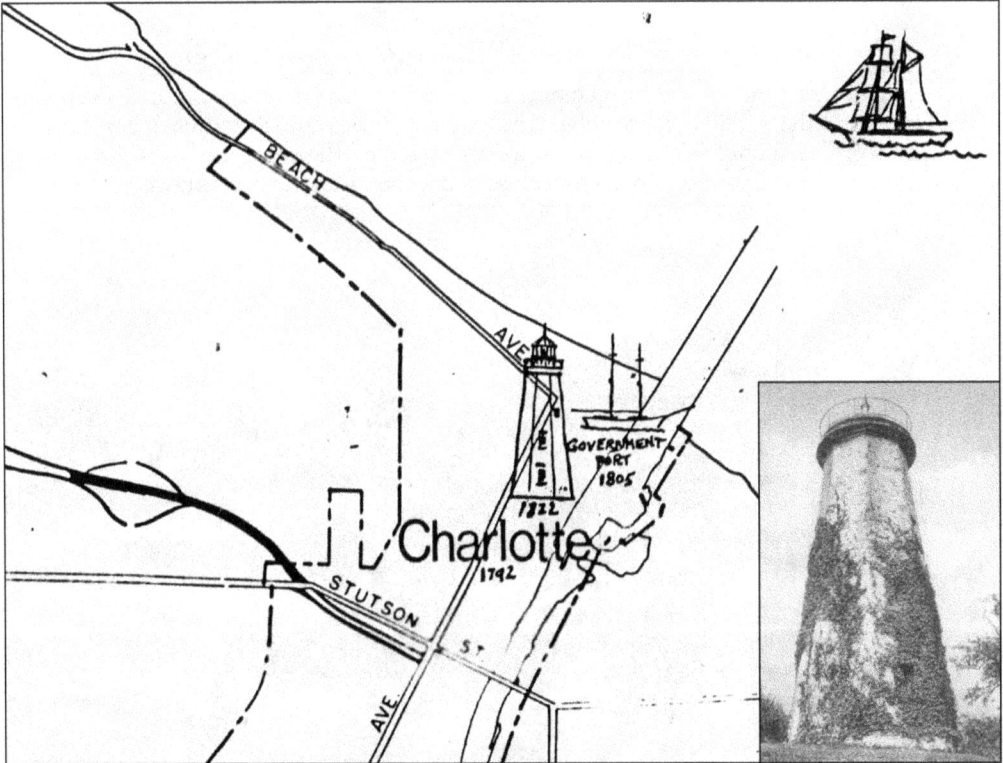

The port of Genesee was established in 1805. Its sturdy stone lighthouse was the first structure in Monroe County to be listed in the National Register of Historic Places (in 1974). It appears in the center of the emblem for the Town of Greece because Charlotte was in Greece when the lighthouse was built in 1822.

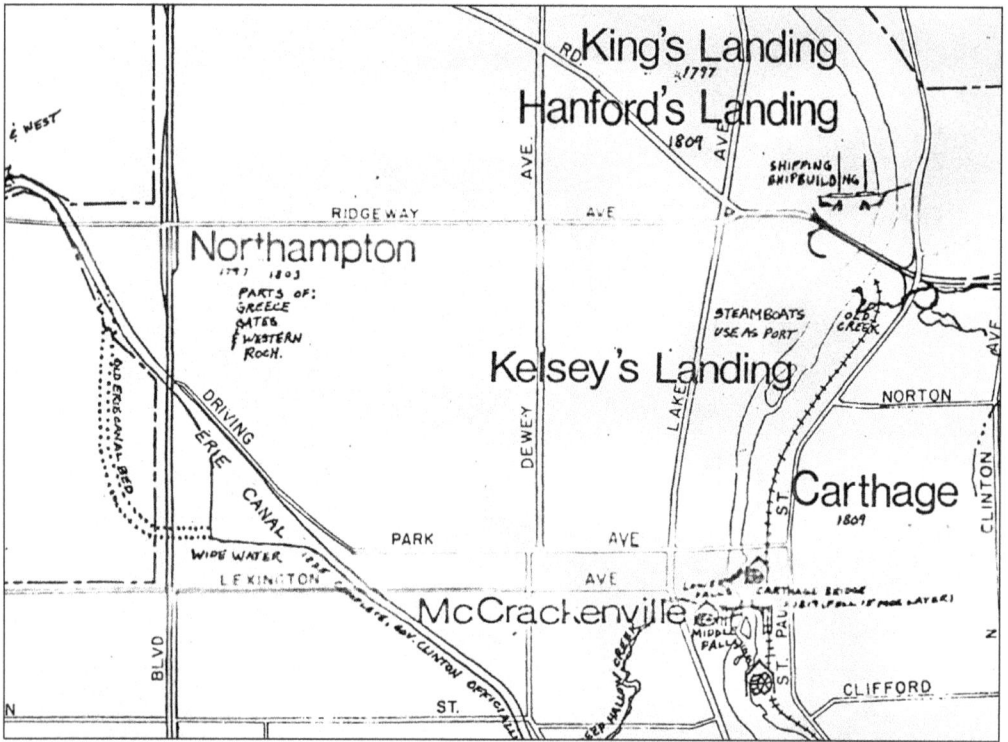

The conjunction of railroads and river commerce made Charlotte grow and prosper. On nearby River Street and the wide boulevard above, riverside bars thrived, and a few manufacturing firms operated. Three churches and a fire station also served the community. By 1900, there were 35 saloons on its 28 street corners, which served a constant stream of tourists.

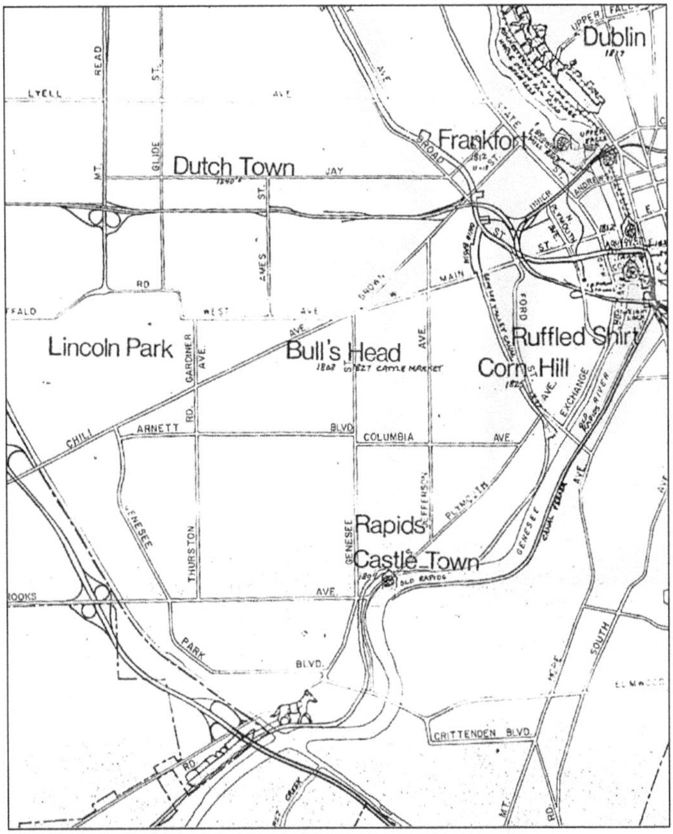

Henry Skinner began constructing a log cabin on the present site of the Powers Building, a humble structure that became the first home in Rochesterville when the Hamlet Scrantom family moved there in 1812. It was re-created on a parade float, pictured below. Hamlet's brother, Henry, later founded Scrantom, Wetmore & Company. Capt. Enos Stone, Colonel Rochester's land agent, purchased the first lot in the new 100-acre tract of land west of the river, but chose to build his home on the east side, near present Stone Street.

FIRST HOME IN ROCHESTERVILLE WAS BUILT IN 1812 BY HAMLET SCRANTOM GRANDFATHER OF THE FOUNDER OF SCRANTOM'S BOOK AND STATIONERY COMPANY

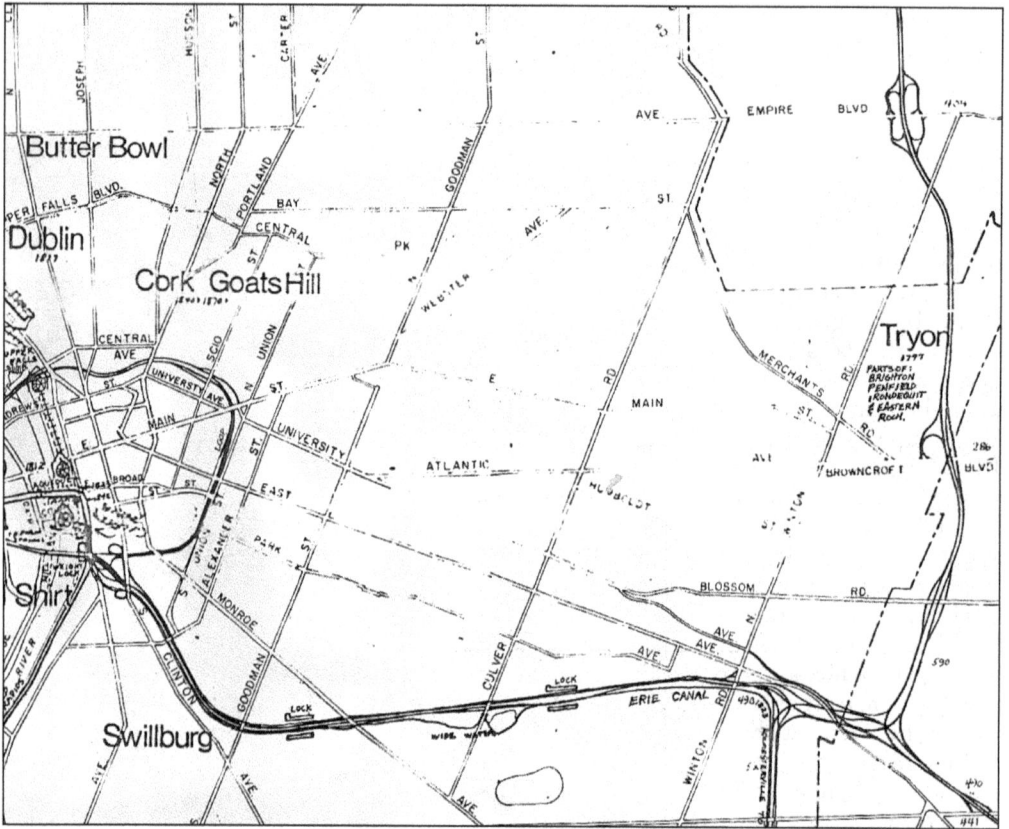

Wilderness forts were established by both the French and the English at Sea Breeze and at Tryon Town in the 18th century. They were disguised as trading posts, but were secretly intended to be used for spying on the activities of the Iroquois Indians. A re-creation of the British Fort Schuyler was built as a Boy Scout project, even though it resembles a fort near Syracuse, not the one at Tryon. Archeologists have determined that the actual location of Fort Schuyler was closer to Irondequoit Bay. The Tryon family later acquired the site and attempted to establish a settlement near Landing Road. On this site was located a store that took hides in trade for merchandise, the only store for miles when the earliest pioneers came. Store ledgers record trades with settlers from as far away as Parma, a distance of more than 25 miles. Irondequoit's first black resident, Asa Dunbar, shipped peaches and other produce from this old bay landing.

Two

FLOUR AND FLOWERS

Genesee Falls, a lithograph by Buford's Litho of New York, shows an Indian-faced rock and a few mills on the east side of the Genesee River. Because the falls impeded navigation, the first settlements sprang up north of the falls at King's Landing and Charlotte. Although the community was called Falltown on an early map, it was destined to bear the name of one of its land proprietors, Nathaniel Rochester. Upriver from Indian Rock, the Rochester Gas & Electric Corporation still utilizes some of the vast waterpower of the river.

The Genesee River Falls in 1836, Rochester, N. Y.
From an old engraving

This postcard reproduced an 1836 engraving, showing the 96-foot-high falls near the Steamboat Landing, below today's Maplewood Park. There, between 1830 and 1860, escaping slaves boarded ships en route to freedom. After Frederick Douglass moved to Rochester in 1847, he was among the abolitionists who were bringing fugitive slaves to the landing.

This view of the splendid falls was published by Raphael Tuck in Holland, purveyors to their majesties, the king and queen of England. This postcard, mailed in 1910, provides a glimpse of the commercial use of the picturesque falls. Mills hugged the riverbanks near Brown's Race in the area now owned by the Rochester Gas & Electric Corporation.

The Driving Park Bridge led crowds across the river to the Driving Park Race Track. There, crowds watched in fascination as racehorses from a wide area competed for awards. McCrackenville, named for its hotel proprietor, lay across Driving Park Bridge on the west bank of the river. The first road surveyed on the west side of the river (1799) led from the McCrackenville and Six Corners area toward King's Landing, then west along Ridge Road to what is now the town of Parma and the Atchinson Settlement, established in 1796.

Close attention paid to the rock formation in this postcard of the bridge area helps one to imagine that Ebenezer Allan, the first miller on the Genesee, is perpetually looking across the river toward the modern mills of his successors. The formation is known as the "Old Man of the Genesee."

One of the many mills along the river bank was purchased by Charles J. Hill, who also served as mayor of the city. The mills were earlier known as the Atkinson and Carthage Mills. Once the building of the Erie Canal provided a way for flour to be cheaply shipped to distant markets, Rochesterville rapidly became a boom town.

This trading card came from A.V. Smith's store at 51 State Street, which specialized in saddles, trunks, and horse fittings. The card lists on its reverse side the July 4, 1882 racing schedule at Driving Park Track: "In the First Race: running half mile heats, Purse $100, $60, $40; Second Race, mile heats, Purse $150, $90, $60; Third Race, one mile heats by three lady drivers, one riding without a saddle; Fourth race, ten miles, $4,000 stake and championship." Miss Pinned and Miss Peek were competing, with not less than eight changes to be made—and they must be made without touching the ground!

The Campbell Whittlesey House was
built in 1835–1836 on Fitzhugh Street.
It is now a museum depicting the
elegant way of life enjoyed by some of
the city's successful millers.

The Jonathan Child House, the home
of Rochester's first mayor, is a landmark
on South Washington Street.

Employees at Harris Seeds on Buffalo Road were typical of the laboring men and female office workers in the area who were employed at the seed, flower, and fruit tree firms that led Rochester to become the Flower City.

Created as a tribute to World War I soldiers, this flag featured a new aster variety named Heart of France in commemoration of the war. The flag was showcased at Vick's seed farm beside the Manitou Road canal bridge and drew throngs of visitors. It was said that a trip to the Flower City without seeing their farms was like a trip to Washington, D.C., without seeing the White House. Vick's acreage was later incorporated into Greece Canal Park.

18

The Brown Brothers Nursery was one of the city's foremost nurseries, specializing in the production of berries and small fruits. The Browncroft area was named in their honor. The elaborate Christmas lights displayed in this subdivision of attractive homes drew crowds of visitors each December. This postcard view shows the gardens of J.K. Hunt on Maplewood Drive, one of the many gardens that graced the Flower City.

John J. Van Zandt's Crescent Mills were among many prosperous mills hugging the river bank. The Van Zandts, descendants of an Albany family, became active in local government. Clarence D. Van Zandt was a mayor, and the Honorable Joanne Van Zandt was the first woman president of the Monroe County legislature. A doctor's wife, Joanne has been active in the program establishing archives at the Rochester General Hospital.

We Roast our Coffees daily, and therefore they are fresher and better than you can get elsewhere.

We make a specialty of PURE and uncolored Teas

Our PURE Baking Powder

will keep good for months, and do what none other will.—TRY IT.

We deal in none but PURE goods, which fact is worthy your consideration.

☞ Sign of the Steaming Tea Kettle. ☜

[OVER]

19

6032, Lilacs, Highland Park, Rochester, N. Y.

This Highland Park postcard shows ladies in Victorian gowns admiring the flowers. Strolling through the park when its first trees and shrubs were newly planted, they are the forerunners of millions who have made springtime pilgrimages to enjoy the park's tulips, magnolias, lilacs, rhododendrons, and pines.

A McCracken Farms carriage passes gorgeous lilac gardens in this scene re-creating the leisurely garden tours of a century ago. Lauren McCracken's Belgian horses are always a big attraction. Sometimes, couples become engaged while riding through the park in this romantic carriage. Later, they may hire the carriage again for a ride on their wedding day.

A vintage postcard printed in Germany shows the park's spectacular pansy bed on Highland Avenue. Victorians believed that gardens should look like carpets lying on the ground. Scrantom, Wetmore & Company published this penny postcard featuring the pansies—an innovation so called because it required a 1¢ postage stamp.

Near the greenhouses on Highland Avenue, where County of Monroe workers grow pansies and various other plants for area parks, Rusty Curtis hauls visitors during one of the annual lilac festivals that attract thousands to view Rochester's flowers each May. More than 500 varieties of lilacs are featured. Lois McCracken is on the right.

At least 5,000 pansy plants are planted in Victorian designs (changed every year) to provide this popular attraction at Highland Park. Other flowers appear in the spring and fall and many a wedding party has posed here for keepsake photographs.

The mounted patrol provided by the Rochester Police Department attracts the interest of Lauren McCracken, Judy Slattery (beside the horse), and other park visitors in this photograph taken at the 1993 Lilac Festival.

Andrew Wolfe, head of Post Publications, one of the state's largest weekly newspaper groups, enjoyed a front-seat ride on this unique double *vis-a-vis* carriage during the 1993 festival parade.

Malcolm and Lauren McCracken built the unusual carriage, perhaps the only twin version existing of the traditional *vis-a-vis* design, in which passengers are seated opposite each other, face-to-face.

The Martin Naparsteck family and Billy Innes enjoy a ride in this lilac time snapshot, as Molly Maguire Naparsteck holds the reins and America Naparsteck looks on. Their guide is Lauren McCracken.

Colgate-Rochester Divinity School's splendid Gothic bell tower is a beautiful sight when glimpsed through the lilacs. This postcard, published by the Manson News Agency, shows a rear terrace surrounded by flowers. From the terrace can be seen what is known as "the million dollar view," a reference to the cost of building the school, originally a Baptist ministers' seminary. It has since merged with several other religious denominations to become an ecumenical training school for religious workers.

This enchanting view of the Mount Hope neighborhood was preserved by Mayor Peter Barry. The mansions of the immigrant Ellwanger and Barry families still grace the avenue adjacent to Highland Park. The beautiful parklands are in an area that was once part of their nursery farm, Rochester's largest. Their nursery stock was shipped worldwide.

This horse-drawn trolley operated by the Rochester City & Brighton Railroad displays an advertisement for jeweler Mose Goodman.

The Frederick Douglass statue has been relocated to Highland Park because of street construction near its original site. Interestingly, this site is in front of a shoe factory, adjacent to the area where President Lincoln spoke briefly from a train passing through Rochester en route to his inauguration. The second Douglass home was located on South Avenue near the park's lily pond, on land now the site of the Patrick Duffy School. There and also at their first home on Alexander Street the Douglass family often sheltered fugitive slaves.

This view of Brooks Avenue looking toward Genesee Street shows the area where early nurseries once flourished and stalwart Quaker residents operated slave stations in their homes, despite the fact that less than 40 percent of the people approved of the Underground Railroad. One of the nurseries there was the Frost family's Genesee Valley Nurseries at 153 Plymouth Avenue, covering over 300 acres near this intersection. Jack Frost of Troy came to Rochester in 1818 to work for Nathaniel Rochester as a landscape gardener. He was paid 75¢ per week.

The Anthony family on Post Avenue was among the abolitionists with Underground Railroad havens in the Genesee Street–Brooks Avenue area. Their famous daughter, Susan Brownell Anthony, has been paid tribute to each year with a commemorative birthday dinner and a procession to her grave in Mount Hope Cemetery.

Susan B. Anthony, Rochester's militant suffragist, is standing in the doorway of her home at 17 Madison Street on this picture postcard. Martha Taylor Howard, succeeded by Roberta Lachiusa and her niece, Lorie Lachiusa Barnum, have inspired the devoted women who helped to save three houses on Madison Street as memorials to Susan B. Anthony and her sisters, Hannah and Mary. Their enlightened work helped to secure voting and educational rights for women.

Women's suffrage did not become a reality until after Susan B. Anthony's death. Politicians were quick to seek female votes; however, it is obvious that Rochester's popular mayor, Hiram H. Edgerton, covered both bases by posing with ladies both for and against women's suffrage. Edgerton developed parks and playgrounds. He also started the public library system and the Rochester Museum, showing an appreciation for culture that was appreciated by many women.

Mayor Samuel Dicker, at the far right, was among the dignitaries in the receiving lines at public receptions held at a downtown hotel every New Year's Day. Judge Clarence Henry, Clarence Smith, and Gordon Howe are also seen among the greeters. Affable Mayor Dicker especially liked to greet the children.

The Bull's Head area, once the site of cattle markets, is dominated by the lovely architecture of the West Avenue United Methodist Church. A plaster bull's head was attached to a nearby store. It was here that Mother Hieronymo O'Brien founded St. Mary's Hospital inside a former stable in September 1857. Only a few of the more than 3,000 Civil War soldiers nursed here by the Sisters of Charity nuns died in the hospital's Soldier's Wing.

St. Mary's Hospital at Bull's Head is shown in this postcard, mailed in 1915. It was Rochester's only hospital until City Hospital, the predecessor of Rochester General Hospital, opened on February 11, 1864—too late to help many soldiers. The Sisters of Charity continued to aid St. Mary's until 2000.

Three

CANAL TOWN

Scrantom, Wetmore & Company issued this postcard of the Erie Canal crossing. Shown is the arched bridge that carried the canal over the Genesee River through an aqueduct. After the canal was rerouted south of the city, the bridge foundation was used for the subway and the Broad Street crossing. Beyond the aqueduct can be seen Court Street Bridge, with the Lehigh Valley Railroad station at the left bank and the Kimball Tobacco Company factory on the right bank. The statue of Mercury races toward the clouds atop its towering smokestack.

OSBURN HOUSE ROCHESTER, N.Y. & View of Genesee River

South Avenue
One Block From
Main St.

The aqueduct shown on this damaged postcard shows canal boats on the present site of the Rundel Memorial Library, a view looking south down South Avenue. The Osburn House Hotel, later the Hotel Milner, was long an area landmark. In this area, near Stone Street, Enos Stone and Elihu Johnson were leaders of a settlement competing with the one begun by Nathaniel Rochester across the river.

Looking west toward the Kimball Tobacco Company's tobacco plant, visible are church spires, the tower of Mercury, and the city hall tower in the distance.

Court St. Bridge over Genesee River, Erie and Lehigh Stations, Rochester, N. Y.

Railroad stations dominated the skyline at the Court Street Bridge when this postcard was made. The Lehigh Valley Railroad station still remains, but the Erie Railroad station area has become a parking lot.

The Court Street dam is shown with the river at flood stage. Before the construction of the Mount Morris dam in Letchworth Park, floods threatened the city; the dams now help prevent the river from flowing over its banks.

This St. Patrick's Day Flood scene appeared in the March 18, 1865 edition of the *Rochester Herald*. The view is from the Main Street Bridge looking west toward the south side, with the courthouse tower in the distance. One of the buildings in the foreground, still standing, housed Frederick Douglass's newspaper and other city publishing plants.

Looking north, Front Street looked like this during the great flood of March 28, 1913.

Shown is the 1913 high-water mark, as seen from the water.

Some smiling gents brave the 1913 flood to pose for a photographer.

This river view looks north along the river and canal beside South Avenue. In the distance is the old weighlock building, where canal boat loads were weighed and paid a toll based on the weight of their freight—a remnant from the days of bustling water transportation, before railroads, automobiles, and airplanes offered more rapid ways to travel.

Named after a stunt jumper who dived to his death over the high falls on Friday the 13th of November 1829, the *Sam Patch* tour boat today takes students and adults on tours of the canal and river, leaving from the new Corn Hill dock. The body of the New Jersey stuntman did not wash ashore until the following St. Patrick's Day, when a Greece farmer named Kedian found him on the riverbank at Charlotte. He was interred in the old Hincher Cemetery at Charlotte, where members of the Hincher family, first pioneers west of the river (1792) are buried.

Riverside tenements demonstrate the constant need for better housing for the poor. As new buildings are erected, areas with older structures eventually become low-rent areas where absentee landlords neglect to improve deteriorating property.

These Brown Street neighborhood billboard advertisements were for milk, paint, and "ready money" loans. Note the wagon at right in this undated photograph. Buildings near the canal were among Rochester's first buildings and were therefore the first to deteriorate after the canal was relocated. The wide canal bed was paved over to become Broad Street. On the street named for early miller and physician Dr. Matthew Brown, a stone warehouse still survives as a towering reminder of the era of huge stone buildings.

The B & O Railroad building is at right in this scene of Broad Street at South Washington Street, near Bull's Head looking west toward Caledonia Avenue and Main Street. Caledonia Avenue was renamed Clarissa Street to honor the wife of Nathaniel Rochester. The Rochester family mansion was on nearby Spring Street, near a natural spring. Flags on the lamp poles indicate that this scene was probably taken around the Fourth of July.

A crowded Main Street can be seen near the Four Corners, where State Street and Exchange intersects Main Street West. Here, trolleys and other vehicles approach a busy intersection, once the main business center of the young, ever-growing city. Some considered it to be "the Young Lion of the West."

The old city hall, an architectural triumph of its time, stood proudly on the north bank of the Erie Canal. The canal is gone and its wide bed became Broad Street, where the building still dominates the corner of Fitzhugh and Broad Streets. Bell ringers made a long, steep climb to the top of its bell tower to ring the bell at midnight on New Year's Eve and other important occasions.

A replica of Court House Square was created in 1934 for the city's "Century on Parade" exhibits. At the old courthouse, located at 39 Main Street West, firemen practiced firefighting by aiming their hoses at the wooden statue of Justice in the tower. Beneath the statue, an observation deck afforded a fine view of the surrounding city. It was demolished to allow for the erection of a larger building. St. Luke's Episcopal church, Rochester's oldest church, stands west of the courthouse. The Rochester family attended St. Luke's.

High electric poles were in place, *c.* 1894, when this photograph was taken on South Fitzhugh Street, looking north at its intersection of Main Street West. The last horse car line is using the middle left lane, while a new electric car line is in the right middle lane. Note the awning on the new Monroe County courthouse at right, now the Gordon A. Howe County Office Building at 39 Main Street West.

In front of the courthouse is the base of the much ridiculed Cogswell drinking fountain. Dr. Henry D. Cogswell, a millionaire dentist in San Francisco, gave public drinking fountains to 31 American cities. Most of the fountains featured a statue of himself, a portly teetotaler, pompously holding aloft a glass of water. After various defamatory substances appeared in the glass, someone (perhaps a wine drinker) removed the statue. One night a wagon pulled up and unidentified thieves spirited away the base as well. Almost everyone rejoiced, even though the prohibition movement was strong in Rochester, thanks to the preaching of the famous fiery evangelist, Rev. Charles Finney.

At the right on Main Street West is the courthouse, shown before the gilded statue of Justice taken from the previous courthouse tower was installed on its front balcony. The Italian Revival building is one of Rochester's finest structures. Following his death, the building was renamed to honor Gordon A. Howe, who presided as Monroe County manager when the courthouse was converted into county offices. Always favoring any improvement that he believed would benefit the people, he greatly expanded county government's support for humanitarian programs during the 42 years of his political career.

On Main Street near Court House Square, a variety of vehicles are shown. This undated view shows the mix of wagons, cars, and streetcars using the roadway. In 1887, the Rochester Railway Company replaced their horse-drawn cars with electric trolleys using overhead lines.

In 1958, on the bicentennial anniversary of Pres. James Monroe's birth, a plaque on the corner of the courthouse is being admired by Clarence Smith, first Monroe County manager; Laurence Gouverneur Hoes, Monroe's great-great-grandson; and Gordon A. Howe, chairman of the board of supervisors. The officers of the Daughters of the American Revolution are proudly wearing their regalia. On the left may be Pearl Smith, who also served as historian for the Irondequoit Chapter of the Daughters of the American Revolution. Their library has been named in her honor.

Two French guests were honored in the summer of 1971, when county medallions were presented to Jean Philippe Kerhoas and Christine Dupuis at the county manager's office during this ceremony remembering POWs and MIAs. The medals were given in recognition of their efforts to assist war prisoners. An effigy of the Eiffel Tower was presented in return. Hon. Joseph Ferrari, president of the Monroe County legislature, and Warren Doremus, whose brother had been a longtime prisoner, were among those present.

Edward A. Frost—the brother of Civil War captain Henry Frost, one of only four Rochester survivors from the 8th New York Cavalry unit that he recruited in Rochester in 1862—supervised the building of this large evergreen arch. It extended from the Reynolds Arcade, where financial contributions to aid escaping slaves were often collected, to the Tallman building on the other side of the street, where Frederick Douglass operated his newspaper, the second black newspaper in the country. Here at the heartland of antislavery sentiment, a number of black spectators were in the crowd on July 4, 1865. Two wounded Zouaves proudly stood on top of the Victory arch during the Fourth of July parade.

State Street buildings appear in this c. 1885 photograph.

43

This view looks down Main Street, c. 1886, from the Reynolds Arcade. There were many lawyers' offices, a photographer, various stores, and the post office in the arcade, one of the country's first indoor shopping malls.

When this photograph was taken in the 1890s, buildings at Four Corners near the Reynolds Arcade were elaborately trimmed with bunting, perhaps for the Fourth of July or Memorial Day.

ain Street, east from State Street, Rochester, N. Y.

Looking east down Main Street from State Street, the tall Chamber of Commerce building is in the distance. The street is filled with streetcars in this postcard view, which was mailed in 1910. Note the old arcade's French-style mansard roof, a design abandoned when the second arcade building was built. The second arcade building was considered to be state-of-the-art and was built in the Art Deco style, popular between 1915 and 1930.

This photograph showing Four Corners was taken before 1895. The West Shore and Pittsburgh depot line has a hard time making the turn because of the crowded conditions. Here was located the "Grand Union," a maze of tracks enabling cars to turn in all directions.

Near the Bausch Building at the Four Corners, c. 1930, men and a horse have hats to help preserve body heat. Six shovelers were apparently assigned to clean snow from one manhole while one irate gentleman seems to be expressing his thoughts to another. (Maybe he was working too fast!)

An advertisement at Four Corners reminds the public to get Saturday's illustrated newspaper.

This trade card advertised McDonald's shoe store, located at 54 State Street.

Happiness is a pair of shoes, at least according to this McDonald's shoe store trade card, showing a fanciful view of happy children. They were made even more so because they were wearing shoes from McDonald's store.

Another trade card is from Eastwood's store at 42 State Street. Rochester was the first city to manufacture infant footwear shaped to a child's foot, an innovation over the old shoes that were cut exactly the same for either foot. Soon, shoe manufacturing was an important local industry where immigrant cobblers excelled in making leather footwear. Frederick Douglass's statue originally stood in a place of honor in front of a shoe factory on Central Avenue.

In addition to shoe making, many residents found employment in the local clothing industry. Working in factories or doing piecework at home was popular work for women and children of very young ages in the era before child labor laws.

This 1896 view of State Street was taken from Main Street at the Four Corners.

This view shows State Street, looking north toward the New York Central railroad overpass, c. 1905–1908. Boland and Austin's Revere Hotel dominates the skyline.

State Street can be seen looking north from the corner of Platt Street, February 11, 1891. One of Rochester's first structures bears a sign identifying it as Leary's Dye House. The Red Rover No. 3 fire engine was once kept in the building by the flagstaff.

The car barn was located at Brown Street and Center Street. When used by busses, not streetcars, a big storage garage was still called a car barn, since tradition dies hard. Even the little horse barns behind private houses that housed automobiles were still called horse barns. Eventually, the autos were also called cars.

The advertisement on the side of this car, c. 1911, announces, "The safest and most economical means of transportation! We have no parking worries!"

In this *c.* 1905 photograph, proud employees of the Rochester Railway Company are looking quite natty in their uniforms. Charles Wellmann is sitting on the right. (Donated by Mary Wellman Marshall.)

This Rochester Railway Company transfer pass shows John Stedman's inventive ticket on which the date, time, sex, age, and general appearance of a rider could be punched by the conductor to prevent cheating. Patented in August 1892, each was good for ten minutes, allowing passengers just enough time to get into another car headed elsewhere on the streetcar line.

A postcard mailed in 1923 shows Eastman Kodak Company's camera works and general offices. The firm continued to expand into several new buildings, and eventually its operations went worldwide, while about 90,000 were employed by the Eastman Kodak Company in the Rochester area. Film was needed for movies and television. The medical and dental professions found film necessary to their success. It was also needed for space exploration and treasured for preserving family memories. Kodak is still the city's largest employer.

The first cathedral, which was built by devout Irish parishioners, stood almost in the shadow of the Eastman Kodak Company. Irish bishop Fulton J. Sheen was a nationally prominent, highly respected Rochester bishop whose television broadcasts were legendary and are still being sold on videotape. He gave more than $10 million to the world's poor and raised many more millions through the Bishop Sheen Fund, now headquartered at 51 State Street. Another popular bishop's energetic efforts to improve parochial schools are remembered today in the name of McQuaid Jesuit High School . Here, Bishop Sheen is conversing with Dr. Eugene "Gene" Bartlett, president of the Colgate-Rochester Divinity School, with which St. Bernard's Seminary later merged.

Shown is Allen Street at State Street, where a manufacturer's outlet sale was "now going on."

This photograph was taken at the curve along the track on Allen Street at Washington Street.

Around 1878, a burned-out building is collapsing after a fire and explosion on Exchange Street's east side, beside the Erie Canal. The ladder truck may belong to the workers attempting to fix a sign on the Columbia Mills Coffee and Spice warehouse. Mustard, cream of tartar, and other spices were advertised.

Exchange Street looked like this in 1889, before the advent of the automobile. Burnett Printing was at the right, one of several printing firms located in that area. Ultimately, Rochester became a printing center. A coffee shop is below the print shop just across the street from the wholesale grocery. Note the many crossbars on the electric poles. On the right corner is the Wilder Building.

56

Shown is Exchange Street, looking south toward the canal bridge. "Old Calamity," another downtown bridge, frequently became stuck, providing workers with a handy excuse for being late for work.

The canal bridge is in the distance in this view of Brown Street. The huge stone warehouse on the left is still standing.

In this 1939 photograph of Main and Exchange Streets, brick pavement was customary and streetcar tracks were everywhere. Although Rochester's "Four Corners" at the intersection of Main and Exchange Streets was the central business area of Nathaniel Rochester's 100-acre tract, another main intersection was at Main Street and Clinton Avenue. This corner became the ultimate hub of activity, in part because large department stores like Sibley's, Edward's, McCurdy's, and the B. Forman Company, plus some smaller clothing stores, including the National, were located there.

New tracks are being laid near South Avenue and Main Street in this photograph.

Four

DOWNTOWN SCENES

This photograph, made for the Rochester Optical Company with a Premo B. Rectilinear lens, looks north toward the county jail on Exchange Street, where confederate captives had been imprisoned during the Civil War. The statue of Mercury, the god of commerce, can be seen in the distance on the Kimball Tobacco Company's chimney tower beside Broad Street. The building at the left is a hotel, and a brick warehouse is on the right.

In front of the city jail at 180 Exchange Street, Sheriff Albert Skinner and other dignitaries pose, surrounded by the county's finest uniformed sheriff's deputies. Skinner was the first to issue uniforms and to use specially painted squad cars. He also had a horse unit because he loved horses and believed that they were the best method of crowd control. A boat patrol was another Skinner touch. During his 38 years as county sheriff, he became a beloved living legend. Once, during a raging blizzard, he walked down a country road in front of a snowplow bringing medication to a sick resident, swinging a lantern so that the plowmen could see where the road was. So powerful was his image that whenever the sheriff entered a banquet room, everyone in the room stood up in respect for him.

Known for his weekly car safaris to Greece and Parma, Sheriff Albert Skinner often purchased baskets of fruit from farmer friends and distributed them to poor families and other acquaintances, including the state's millionaire governor, Nelson Rockefeller. Gordon Howe is looking on. He and the taciturn bachelor sheriff went almost everywhere together.

Near the Civic Center, National Guard members appear ready, willing, and able to help with crowd control, as County Manager Gordon Howe has come to inspect them. They were alerted and remained on duty at the Culver Road armory when the city was threatened by riots in 1964. The militia and sheriff's deputies were not used, however, to avoid exacerbating the situation. On July 2, 1964, in response to numerous acts of civil unrest across the nation, Pres. Lyndon B. Johnson signed the historic Civil Rights Act.

The old penitentiary, where Abraham Lincoln had pardoned several prisoners, grew decrepit and was finally demolished. The land was soon given over to a better use; the site now is filled with festival tents at lilac time. Here is located a small band shell and the Vietnam Veterans Memorial. Adjacent to the Cornell Cooperative Extension's farm and home center is the remnant of the old prison cemetery, a Potter's Field where criminals and occupants of the county's poorhouse, shown above, were buried.

The penitentiary farm gave prisoners who were trustees an opportunity to work outside in the fresh air.

It is feeding time at the public trough in this photograph of the penitentiary pig farm and its outbuildings. Pigs, cows, and vegetables were raised, providing good food supplies to be used in the prison kitchens.

After the farm operation ended, the county used the land for a new community college. This 1969 picture of the Monroe Community College's board of directors shows, from left to right, the following: (seated) attorney Hollenbeck, Kent Damon, Leonard Tomczak, J.D. Crino, Marion Folsom, secretary Caroline Weston, Alexander Gray, County Manager Gordon Howe, Carl Hallauer, Alice Young, and Dr. Sam Stabbins; (standing) Miss Brennan, Joseph Ferrari (president of the Monroe County legislature), Dr. Leroy Good (college president), and two student representatives.

The effects of poverty, illness, and alcoholism posed many problems, but many Jewish and Christian leaders made efforts to help them. Among these efforts were those of the Salvation Army, the Open Door Mission, Catholic charities, and the Peoples Rescue Mission, operated by the Richards family, father and son. Shown is a new children's playground area beside the Front Street rescue mission, hardly an attractive or safe place for children to play.

Rattlesnake Pete and Frog Legs George were among the beloved "characters" of the 19th century. George sold frog legs at the public market. Peter Gruber happily welcomed customers to his Front Street bar and museum of weird curiosities, sometimes wearing a suit entirely made out of shiny black snakeskins. The suit has been preserved by the Rochester Museum and Science Center.

Shown is Andrews Street at Front Street. Front Street was a colorful waterfront street later noted for a clutter of sidewalk merchants, fast bargains, and cheap walk-in rooms, where migrants and derelicts of all types could find overnight lodging for a quarter or less. A social worker described the upstairs rooms as "nothing but stalls."

PERFUMED WITH

AUSTEN'S

FOREST FLOWER COLOGNE

J. FAHY & CO.,

DEALERS IN

Millinery and Fancy Dry Goods,

Nos. 60, 62, 64 State, 2, 4, 6 Market, and 27 29 and 31 Mill Streets.

ROCHESTER, N. Y.

AGENTS FOR

AUSTEN'S FOREST FLOWER COLOGNE

The most fashionable perfume of the day.

Each purchaser of a bottle of this Cologne will be given a beautiful Japanese handkerchief.

This trade card from Fahy's store features a lovely romantic scene on the front, plus an offer no one could resist—a free Japanese handkerchief with cologne priced at only 50¢ or 75¢ a bottle. Their hats and other "dry goods" merchandise was available on State, Market, and Mill Streets.

65

This photograph of the northwest corner of Front Street at Andrews Street shows that Fahy's market operation had expanded into several buildings. This area was the hub of the west side until the business center eventually moved on eastward. Buildings along the Main Street Bridge between Front and Water Streets were eventually removed because they became fire hazards; in time, Front and Water Streets were also in need of urban renewal.

A hotel delivery wagon is outside 37–43 Front Street. Here, butter sold for 23¢, bacon for 17¢, milk for 9¢, bread for 16¢, and hams for 9¢ or 13¢ per pound. Coney Island may claim to have originated the red hot dog, but one lasting legacy of Rochester's meat-packing operations was the Russer family's invention of white hot dogs—often called "porkers" because the addition of larger amounts of pork gave the sausage links their white color. They are sometimes frozen and shipped by air to Florida for the enjoyment of transplanted Rochesterians whose mouths water for a good old "porker".

Shown is the corner of Front Street and Central Avenue, with the Bracket House hotel and Congress Hall in the distance. Frederick Douglass and Susan B. Anthony spoke there. Note the electric poles, carrying one insulator for each customer line. The Flower City Plant Food Company and J.C. Nugent & Company occupied part of the block also used by the Maine Manufacturing Company, a firm dealing in fruit tree sprayers, force pumps, and pipe cleaners. A paper box specialty company was conveniently located next to J.C. McMaster's infant shoe business.

Translations of the famous "Rochester Rappings" of the Fox Sisters, later thought to be a hoax, inspired a host of efforts to communicate with the dead. The Spiritualist Church was an outgrowth of the Fox phenomenon. These girls look like they might be holding a seance, but it is more likely that they are playing with a Ouija board. The Postal Portrait Company, 66 North Street, published this postcard but did not explain what was happening. Maybe it was just a tea party or one girl's face reflected in several mirrors.

This trade card promotes Dr. Mettaur's headache pills, obviously wonderful for babies. Maybe not, but they were advertised as "good for man and beast" and probably helped—since most of them included heavy doses of alcohol, as did Horatio Warner's Safe Cure. Besides its role as a patent medicine center, other factories in the city produced perfume, eye glasses, thermometers, water heaters, hardware, dental equipment, radio and car parts, candy, canned foods, shoes, neckties, belts, buttons, and other clothing. Italian and Jewish tailors found their talents desirable and important to the industry.

Mr. Aikenhead offered reimbursement for tallow and grease at his Front Street establishment. This 1905 photograph showing 60 Front Street illustrates the 19th-century proclivity for recycling. Fats could be used to make soap and candles. A similar trade situation existed at Michael Jackson's State Street implement business, which accepted used scrap metal, allowing farmers to trade their refunds toward tools or "land size," a form of fertilizer. Among the customers doing so was one of the forebears of Pres. George Bush. Some members of the Rochester and Penfield Bush families were active abolitionists.

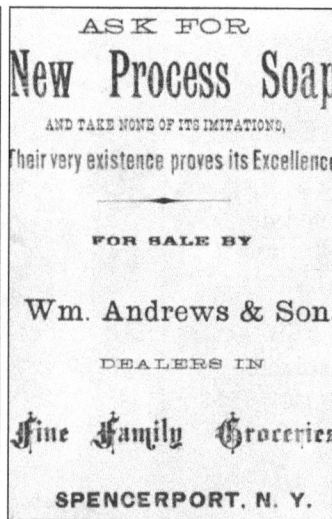

Shown is the front and back of a trade card for a wonderful 3-pound bar of New Process soap, on sale by William Andrews & Son, dealers in fine family groceries at Spencerport, New York. This was the "new and improved" version for which the Buffalo manufacturer claimed there were no imitations. The Rochester Soap Works provided local employment opportunities.

Sidewalk sales by Front Street clothiers often cluttered the sidewalks and storefronts with racks of inexpensive clothes available to derelicts and anyone else desiring a real bargain. If no one was looking, a derelict might help himself to some free "duds."

At an unknown location, an enterprising merchant operated this combination grocery and soda fountain.

The old New York Central Railroad station on Central Avenue is shown on this postcard..

A new station with windows built to resemble train wheels was later built, shown in this postcard view.

The public market near Central Avenue made it possible for farmers in Irondequoit and Greece to market their fresh produce to city dwellers or ship it elsewhere. Although its market gardens have almost vanished, a north–south transportation pattern still exists in Irondequoit—a reminder of the influence that the fresh food market and the wealth of jobs available in the city played in developing Irondequoit when the children of immigrants who worked in the city moved north.

The market scene is similar today, except that the horses and wagons have been replaced by trucks and vans. An earlier marketplace was the old hay market on the west side of the river at Front Street on the waterfront, offering provisions for animals and other farm products to a bargain-seeking public. From the waterfront playground and sandy beach at Front Street, a string of buildings and open-air market stalls also offered a variety of goods along the Main Street Bridge. Haggling for reduced prices was customary.

Nothing could be more adorable than this snapshot of a child sitting on a curb near a former Jewish synagogue. The Baden-Kelly-Ormond Street area, street names revealing their ethnic origins, later became home to many African Americans as the children of immigrants moved to newer residences creating a metro sprawl. Middle-class families often moved to nearby Greece, Chili, Webster, or Henrietta; upper-class citizens frequently went to Brighton, Pittsford, Perinton, or Mendon.

The Dunbar Red Cross Unit was one of several women's charitable organizations working to advance community assistance programs. During the Civil War, a Negro Women's Anti-Slavery Society was organized, holding bazaars and other fundraising events to help runaway slaves escape or purchase their freedom.

The Central Avenue Bridge is shown in this picturesque view, showing the city's busy railroad traffic. The railroad was important for fast travel and quick shipments of goods, but was a real threat to the slower-moving canal boats. Because of the opposition of the railroad interests in the Chamber of Commerce, the canal was eventually rerouted south of the city. It was successfully argued that purchase of already developed downtown land for expansion would be very costly and the many raised canal bridges downtown slowed up street traffic.

The canal weighlock, where canal boats were weighed and charged fees, is seen in this June 5, 1922 view beside the river, near South Avenue and the Court Street dam. Subway tracks are being laid beside the weighlock. The canal was rerouted through Genesee Valley Park, and other new transportation programs brought hard paved macadam roads; many were built throughout the county during the Good Roads Program of 1931.

Underneath Broad Street, a portion of the old subway that ran atop the canal aqueduct at the base of Broad Street Bridge can be seen during the construction process in the 1920s. Vandalism, fires unintentionally set by vagrants and secret witchcraft ceremonies, made its abandoned sections a source of public concern after the subway closed. Here in peaceful isolation sometimes slept some of Rochester's homeless, the poorest of the poor.

The Rundel Memorial Library was under construction when this photograph showing the foundation wall of the library was taken, c. 1934. The library was built beside the Genesee River at the spot that had been the Native Americans' fording place. The bedrock close to the surface, on which horses and people could easily cross, can be seen in the foreground. Looking east between Broad Street and Court Street, the tower of the Seneca Hotel can be seen in the left distance, as well as the Osburn House hotel and other buildings along South Avenue, originally called South St. Paul Street after the church named for St. Paul.

This photograph was taken looking west over the Court Street Bridge. At the left is the Erie Railroad station, and beyond it the National Casket Company, where Pres. Ulysses S. Grant's casket was made. At right is the Tudor-style Kimball Tobacco factory where shirts, cigars, and cigarettes were once made. The War Memorial and Blue Cross Arena now occupies the Kimball site and the WWI Peace Dove memorial statue has been relocated beside it.

Police parade by the German Insurance Building on Main Street West at Court House Square. After their helmet style was changed in 1915, Rochester's police no longer resembled British "bobbies."

This WWI-era scene features Victory Loan guards displaying their Coast Artillery cannon in a patriotic parade down Main Street.

As new forms of transportation helped the city to grow, traffic accidents and criminal offenses required the police services offered by neighborhood precincts. Protecting additional buildings required more firemen. New schools, churches, and places of business were needed and many neighborhood stores prospered. A precious landmark still remains: after fire destroyed the interior of St. Joseph's Catholic Church, its magnificent facade was retained as a focal point in a little downtown park dedicated at the time of Rochester's 1984 sesquicentennial, when the Honorable Thomas Ryan was mayor. This is a view of North Clinton at Franklin Street looking north, c. 1979. In the foreground are advertisements for children's shoes, the Adam Men's Studios, featuring hairpieces for men and women, and Kipling's store, where hats, wigs, and bags were offered for sale at the city's best hat shop. Brodsky's advertisement, painted on a sidewall, reminded customers to visit their popular yard goods store on Joseph Avenue. Piehler's unabashedly proclaimed themselves as the No. 1 car sales lot. The central attractions of Rochester remained at the Main Street area until late in the 20th century, when shopping plazas, especially those in the neighboring towns of Greece and Irondequoit, drew many customers away from the heart of the city.

In 1935, Franklin Jones's little auto sales lot at 721 Alexander Street was apparently a good place for a bargain since America was on wheels, with "a car in every garage." Even in rural areas, fewer and fewer horses were seen on the streets, since a family "flivver" was easier to care for and cheaper to maintain.

Automobile trouble, then, as now, was sometimes not with the car but with the driver. This spectacular scene at an unidentified location came from the Mitchell collection at the Parma Town Hall.

At the Bay Street Stadium (above) or Silver Stadium on Norton Street, crowds enjoyed the sport of champions. Billy Graham's revivals drew large crowds as did other events offered at Redwing Stadium, often called Silver Stadium in tribute to the Silver family's long struggle to provide a fine stadium for the home team. Night games became possible with the introduction of electricity.

The Edgerton Park Stadium (above) was similar to those on Bay and Norton Streets. A more modern structure was the Holleder Stadium, named to honor the famous West Point football player Donald Holleder of Rochester. It hosted football games, marching band competitions, and other events. It also provided a headquarters for fundraising walks for charity. While building nearby Ridgeway Avenue, skeletons of Native Americans who appeared to have been almost 7 feet tall were found buried near an old Native American campsite at a spring by Weiland Road. They might have become wonderful athletes had they lived in the 20th century.

On August 12, 1913, Clinton Avenue North, seen from Catharine Street, was the place to buy some Rochester ice cream.

Clinton Avenue is seen in this view looking north from Main Street near the Odd Fellows building. The Odd Fellows is a fraternal organization that accepts members from all professions.

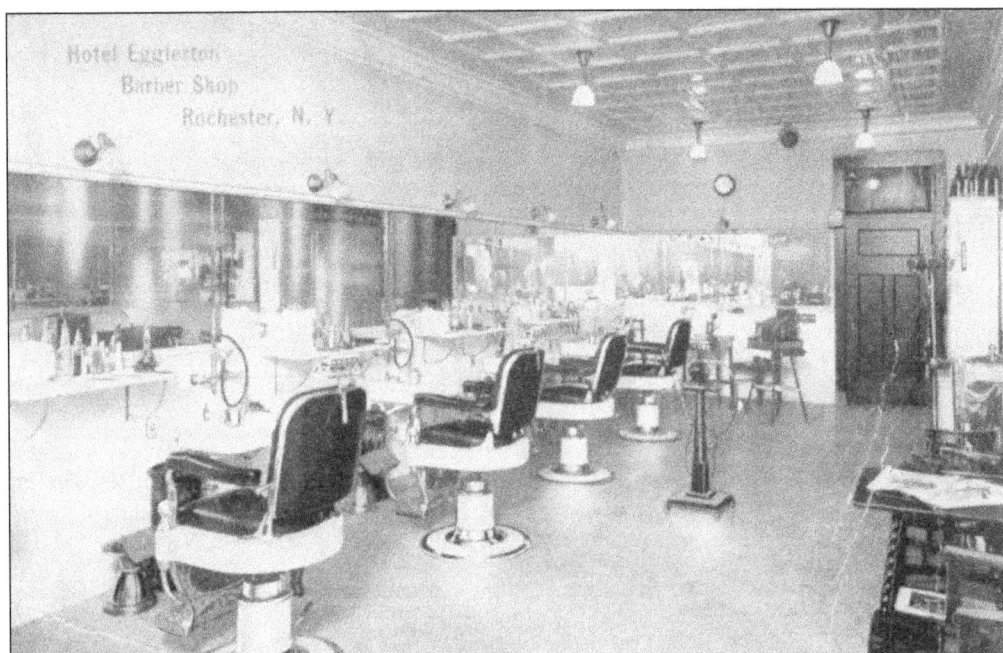

"Four chairs, no waiting!" was the message of a postcard from the Hotel Eggleston's barbershop, with its lovely stamped tin ceiling. For the ladies, trainees in the Harper Method of beauty culture or the Continental School of Beauty would happily fix your hair for a very small charge, as they practiced doing hair dressing and manicures.

At the Hotel Rochester, a lavish interior with potted palms, maroon velvet furniture, marble columns, attractive golden chandeliers, rich, paneled ceiling, telephone booths, and iron grillwork included eager waiters hoping to serve you in the rear dining room. How prim and proper, and there is not a lady in sight!

Traffic delays were customary at Main Street intersections in the city's busiest shopping area, where crowds often jammed the streets. This is a November 1923 picture showing Main and Clinton Streets. It is reproduced courtesy of the New York State Museum of Transportation. Fine suits were $35, and overcoats were $25. This downtown scene portrays Rochester's bustling business section before WWI. Support for the war effort was strong and probably grew even stronger during WWII, when the war affected the homelands of countless local immigrants. Many local men and women were in service. Those stationed in Italy came home with a wonderful new business idea: pizza parlors.

This undated photograph of Clinton Avenue North shows the Weis & Fisher Company store, "household outfitter," long a respected furniture and carpet emporium.

Sam Gottry was the well-known proprietor of a local carting company with offices in the Wilder Building at the Four Corners. This postcard for the company shows its work horses. Throughout the 19th century, many such worthy animals hauled all sorts of items through the streets in wagons. They also sped tanks of water to fire scenes, drew hearses and beer wagons, hauled dirt for construction crews, and aided farmers with plowing and field cultivation.

An oyster lunch was only one of the attractions, *c.* 1885, in the area where East Avenue enters Main Street at Franklin Street Square. The building in back of S.D. Millman's store became the Sibley Block after the disastrous Sibley Fire of 1904.

Franklin Square in the WWI era featured both Chinese food and a variety menu at Buckley's Triangle Cafe on the triangle of streets that formed the square. At right is the Baptist church, predecessor of the Baptist Temple building. A new Liberty Pole now stands in the square, a glorious sight when decorated with holiday lights.

Main Street, c. 1931, as seen from East Avenue, looking west on Main Street by the triangle at North Street, was once the site of patriotic Liberty Poles, but is now the home of the ultramodern pole resembling a ship's sail. The Sibley, Lindsay, and Curr store and clock tower is at the right. McCurdy's store is at the left. Beyond McCurdy's are the Hotel Seneca and the tower of the Lincoln Alliance Bank. Also at the right is the tower of the Powers Building at the Four Corners. Stores on the triangle include Becker's Glasses, a shoe store and beauty shop featuring the latest "hairdos." At Christmastime, everyone visited the Christmas Tunnel exhibited at Sibley's, ogled the toys and electric trains, and watched the kazoo player. E.W. Edwards's store featured Madame Alexander dolls and a miniature train ride. Note the on-street parking.

The Sibley Fire of 1904 destroyed the old Sibley block farther west on Main Street.

French tailoring and a reasonable price ensured that style and value were always associated with the McCurdy family's stores. Midtown Plaza, the first indoor shopping plaza built in America over a parking garage, was conceived and built through Forman and McCurdy's leadership to provide an opportunity to shop without going outside in Rochester's inclement weather. Its musical Clock of the Nations was a great attraction, even though it was frequently out of order. It stood in an indoor public square that was often crowded, especially when parents brought children to see the plaza's towering Christmas tree, visit Santa Claus and Mrs. Claus on their Magic Mountain and ride the monorail.

This postcard view of South Clinton from Main Street looks toward the bank and the Hotel Seneca. Note the four percent interest rate offered by the bank.

Behind the savings bank on the left corner in this view of South Clinton Avenue crossing Main Street is the Universalist church. Farther south is the Lyceum Theater, where the performances might have sometimes irritated less liberal congregations.

Shown is the Victoria Theater on Clinton Avenue South, with the Hotel Seneca on the right.

Women demonstrate outside the Roxy Theater, which later became "the Embassy," a burlesque house on South Avenue. Jessie Bonesteel and many other famous stars performed there in its earlier days. Jessie was thought to be one of the best actresses Rochester ever produced. A Greece native, actress, and drama coach who supposedly coached Gregory Peck and other actors, Jessie later changed her name to Jessica Bonstelle. Don Rickles is another local talent who has achieved success in comedy roles, as has Foster Brooks, who likes to vacation in nearby Mendon. Actress Louise Brooks starred as the first Betty Boop before going into retirement at Rochester.

Before it was paved, Lake Avenue near Kodak was full of mud puddles. The Wehle Bakery truck parked in front of the A & P store recalls memories of their delectable "hermit cookies," made from oatmeal, raisins, spice, nuts, and a bit of culinary magic. Free crystal was given away to ladies at Friday matinees at the Lake Theater. Note the awnings.

The Lyceum Theater is seen at the right. Rochester's most impressive movie theater, the RKO Palace, had an elegant interior and lavish furnishings that can never be forgotten. Happy children saw *Snow White* and *The Wizard of Oz* at one of the big city theaters. Sadly, Lowe's, the Paramount, Capitol, Lyceum, and other theaters became victims of the television age, and most of them have been demolished. Small bisque figurines made from former Rochesterian Maud Humphrey's sketches of winsome children are still being sold. Some people like to imagine that they resemble her son, Humphey Bogart, one of the 20th century's most popular movie stars.

The Elite Marching Club marched proudly in a parade welcoming athlete Jessie Owens on October 14, 1936.

These Polish dancers appeared at an Exposition Park show in 1920. Their sense of rhythm, cooking skills, artistic excellence, friendly camaraderie, and devout religious spirit endeared the Polish community to many. Polish, German, Jewish, Irish, and Italian neighborhoods brought an international flavor to the streets north of the downtown business area. In the 1950s, many Puerto Ricans who were seeking economic advantage came to the area.

The Auditorium Theater, built by the Free and Associated Masons at 875 East Main Street, provides the group with meeting rooms, plus a source of revenue from the stage and auditorium that is frequently used for traveling stage shows, plays, musicals, and other performances. At a ceremony there, Gordon Howe and Albert Skinner were honored by the Lalla Rookh Grotto lodge. Monarch Sweeting is in the center of this photograph. The Grotto is a social organization for Master Masons who meet together to enjoy friendly fellowship and share happy occasions.

George Eastman's splendid East Avenue mansion and the humble little home where George Eastman was born have now become a part of a film museum and preservation center surrounded by formal gardens. In Eastman's time, organists were hired to play the mansion's pipe organ while Eastman, his mother, and friends dined in style.

Eastman never lived to hear some of the great performers that his music school helped to train. Mitch Miller often expressed his appreciation for his training at the Eastman School. As band leader for Fred Whiting and his Pennsylvanians, he became nationally famous. Chuck Mangione and his cousin, Gap Mangione, led successful bands that made the Mangione name well known, blending elements of classical and jazz music into a new musical style. Jerre Mangion became a highly respected author and teacher, often praised for his folk stories of life and customs in the home of his Sicilian parents, the Gaspar Mangiones of Cole Street. Cab Calloway was another Rochesterian who became a nationally known singer, and there were numerous others. Garth Fagan and Olive McQue's dance students often excelled in stage performances.

94

It cost 2¢ to mail this Rochester News Company postcard in 1927. The Eastman Theater was one of George Eastman's many gifts offered to improve the community. Tone deaf, Eastman had the theater built to honor his mother's love for music. It is said that he incorporated her initial (K for Katherine) into the name of his business. Reportedly, some imagine that he still makes ghostly visits to the seat he had always occupied in the Eastman Auditorium.

Eastman's legacy has helped to develop Rochester into a community that deeply appreciates music. The Eastman School of Music has grown to include 1,000 students and 250 teachers—so large that a 25 percent reduction is now believed necessary. The Hockstein Music School also has nearly 1,000 students.

William Warfield, best known for his performance of "Old Man River" in the movie *Showboat,* and his first wife, opera singer Leontyne Price, have long been appreciated for their musical abilities, which "Bill" has transferred into teaching in his later years. A scholarship at the Eastman School bears his name—a name also highly revered in Rochester because his father and brother led local church congregations.

Abraham Lincoln's statue stands in Washington Square Park atop a memorial to Civil War soldiers and sailors. The park was so named because in its early days, when landowners on both sides of the river competed to establish a city, both Nathaniel Rochester and Elisha Johnson had each designated areas for a courthouse. After Nathaniel Rochester's political ties helped him to achieve success in placing the courthouse on his west side plot, the east side plot was unused, so it became a park named in honor of the nation's first president. Court Street retained its name even though the courthouse was not built on it.

On May 3, 1933, survivors of Company K of the 13th New York Volunteers held their 72nd reunion and honored Fayette C. Batcheller of Shortsville, New York. A faint arrow points to Batcheller, who is standing in the fourth row at the right, near the 1892 Soldiers and Sailors Monument. This 50th anniversary reunion photograph was taken in 1911. Local residents were greatly shocked in June 2000 when the grave of the men's commanding general, Gen. Elisha G. Marshall, was desecrated and his skull stolen.

On the south side of Washington Square was Convention Hall, a Victorian equivalent of today's convention center and a showplace of its time. Many activities were held there. Scrantom's published this postcard, which was mailed in 1924. Earlier, when the postage was only 1¢, they were called penny postcards. The name stuck, despite the rise in postage rates.

This postcard, mailed in 1924, notes that the Rochester Business Institute, founded in 1863, had an enrollment of over 1,700 when this picture of a July summer class was taken at Washington Square. It noted that students from over 40 states and foreign countries attended classes in the 1915 fireproof building at 172 Clinton Avenue South, opposite Washington Square.

D. Deavenport & Company on Franklin Street was one of many merchants with trucks to deliver butter, eggs, and fruit.

During this WWI victory parade, jubliant marchers on October 12, 1918, had a handmade sign that happily proclaimed, "We got the Kaiser in the cage!"

Religious articles and pictures were available near Boston Lunch on the corner of Franklin Street and Clinton Avenue North. This photograph is undated, but is probably from the 1920s.

In this photograph taken on March 3, 1900, a fire engine is in the high snowbank on East Avenue in front of the Cutler Building. The Cutler mail chute was one of many Rochester inventions. Lake-effect snow—caused when air warmed by Lake Ontario's water collides with cold air blowing south from Canada—often results in snowbanks several feet deep. But take heart—spring is only about a week away.

This summer scene looks northwest on East Avenue.

This bucolic 1934 view of East Avenue, the "street of many mansions," was published in the 1934 *Centennial History*. Known for its beautiful trees, the street's mammoth homes are gradually being converted into apartments. Much of the city is filled with inexpensive 1920s housing. In older areas, the main cause of serious riots in disadvantaged residential areas was discontent because of the need for schools, jobs, and better housing for the poor. Better schools remain a constant challenge, but improving them has been a goal of Mayor William Johnson.

Five

GROWTH AND RENEWAL

After the former Western House of Refuge moved to Rush in 1911 and became the State Industrial School of Industry, its former buildings were remodeled and the 45 acres of grounds were converted into Edgerton Park. It was named in honor of Mayor Hiram Edgerton, but was also known as Exposition Park. The Manson News Agency published this postcard featuring an aerial view of the park near Dewey Avenue and a new grandstand built by the Rochester Work Bureau in 1934, largely funded by federal grants. It replaced the 1913 wooden grandstand, which was weathered, in need of repairs, costly to maintain, and so situated that the sun shone in the audience's eyes. The new steel structure faced south, with seating for 4,024 people. Similar to another grandstand at Red Wing Stadium, it included 280 tons of structural steel and 11,400 rivets. There was also a quarter-mile cinder running track, a football field, and other athletic facilities.

The Rochester Exposition was a popular annual event. Large conventions, exhibits, horse races, fairs, and shows of all kinds were also held at Exposition Park. The National Flower and Garden Show, a horticultural exhibit, and car shows were especially popular. Mothers of service personnel paraded there on September 4, 1918, at a "Defender of Liberty Day" observance, shown above. There was a war garden exhibit in the tent.

The Amazing Horse Tower was a construction that might offend some today. But watching horses jump had long been a featured event at public horse shows. Breeders of fine saddle horses and jumpers from some of the finest stables competed in an annual horse show.

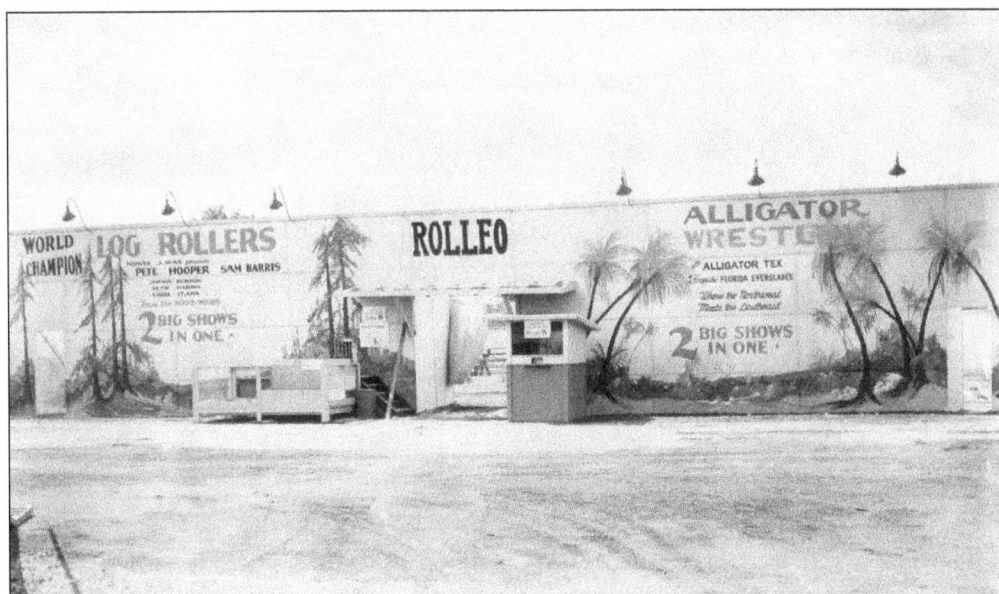

The Midway, a feature of the city's centennial celebrations, included a "rolleo" with world champion log rollers and "Alligator Tex," the alligator wrestler. In the midst of a serious national period of economic depression, the shows at Exposition Park were spirit-lifting events, as were the many playground programs held in city parks.

The Great Depression brought a lack of jobs and money all across America. Gordon Howe headed the county's Works Progress Administration (WPA) program, which poured thousands of dollars into "make work" projects to improve highways, bridges, schools, public buildings, and parks. Unskilled women were employed in a WPA comforter factory, where three women could tie a comforter in 12 minutes. In this 1935 photograph, most of the ladies are wearing aprons. The men apparently are supervisors.

Food shortages were also common during the Great Depression. In farming areas where families could grow their own food, many families survived by eating mostly potatoes, turnips, dumplings, or pancakes, selling the rest of their produce to make ends meet. For hungry families, WPA food commissaries were quite important. Men in the meat-wrapping department for the county's commissaries were busily at work, wearing dress shirts, ties, hats, and suits—but no sanitary rubber gloves.

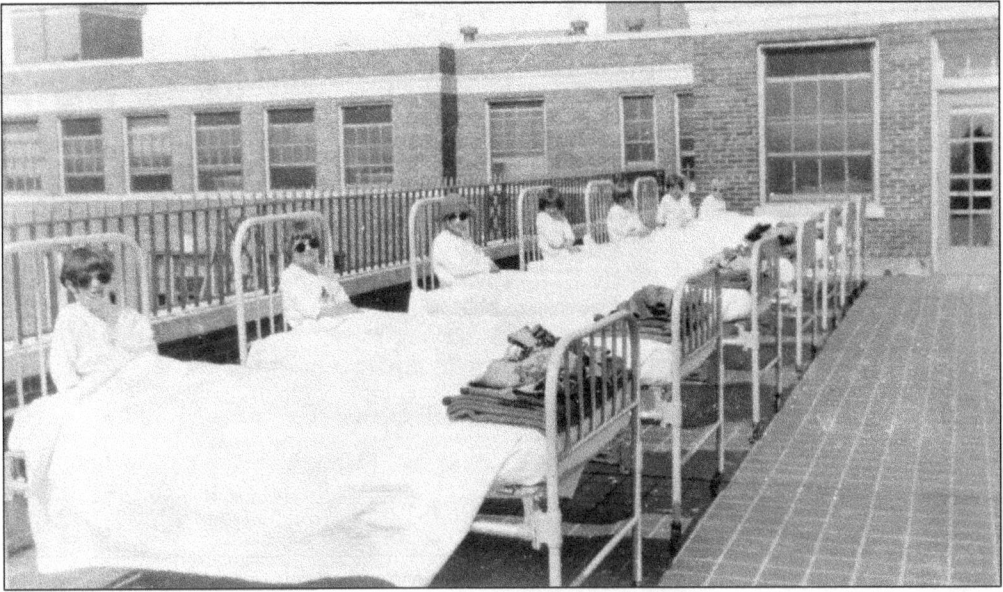

As the scourge of tuberculosis threatened thousands, Iola Sanitarium treated sick children by placing their beds on an outside terrace (above), where they could be exposed to fresh air. Forced to play in the snow wearing only their underwear (below), they either died from pneumonia or built up enough endurance to survive. Although miracle medicines and inoculations successfully changed treatment, a few cases of tuberculosis still continue to break out every year.

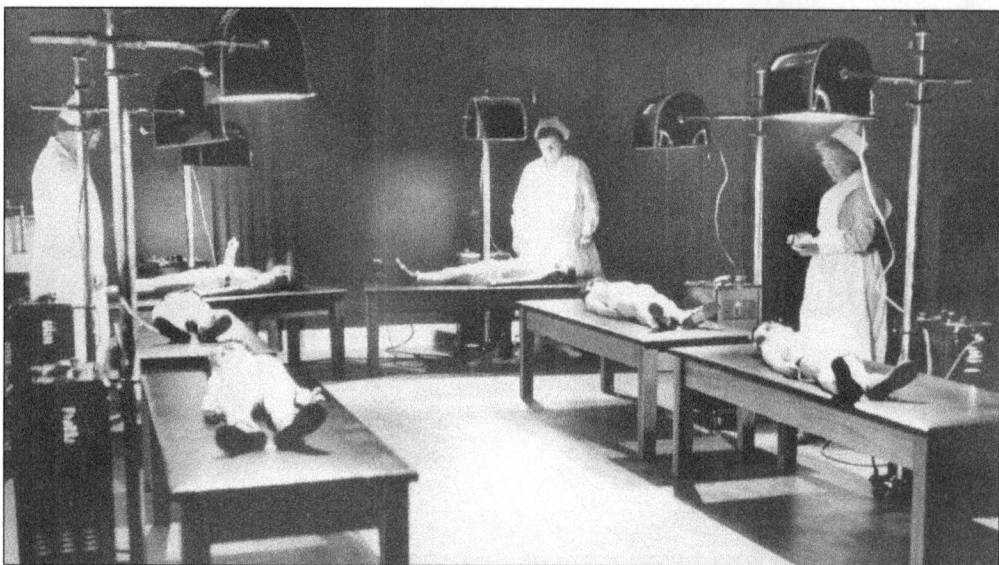

Three nurses wearing the traditional white caps and uniforms supervise six little patients as they lie on hard tables under sunlamps. How easily they could have rolled off onto the floor!

The Iola Schoolroom was where classes were offered for the resident patients. Scientific mapping of the genomes in the body's 10 trillion cells is now expected to provide a road map that may provide an understanding of the inherited genetic causes of disease. This knowledge would eventually prevent the spread of infectious diseases such as the ones that devastated children in the past.

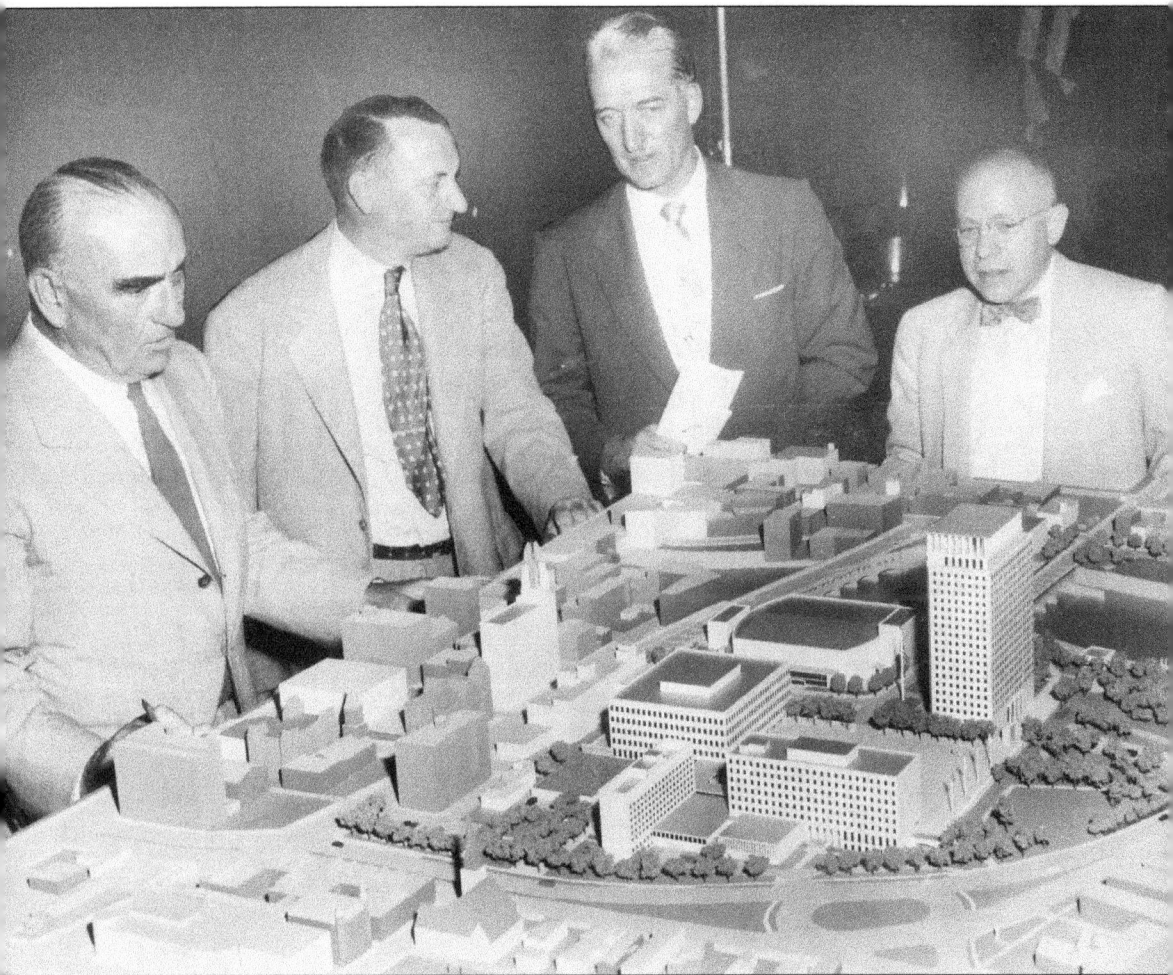

Admiring a model of the new Civic Center in 1956 are the following: Perry Smith, a New York architect; Donald Faragher, a Rochester architect; Gordon Howe, chairman of the Board of Supervisors, and Hyman B. Freeman, city councilman. Plans for a tall city-county office building there and an overpass over Exchange Street were eventually scrapped. Although a new building was planned on the adjacent plaza, the plaza remained a concrete wasteland, even though Governor Rockefeller had promised Howe that money to build would be forthcoming. It was 1999 before a new county structure was built (at a different location) and the plaza site was transferred to the City of Rochester for a new public safety building.

Having outgrown their previous quarters at 39 Main Street West, court operations and both the city and county jails were moved into severely plain modern buildings in the new Civic Center Plaza. By the end of the 20th century, four new buildings were needed. By then, the main public offenses were not alcoholism and thefts—drug offenders comprised the bulk of the prison population, and the number of murders in the city had sharply escalated. Also, a bit of history was lost forever: the home of Winston Churchill's Jerome grandparents had stood in the area used for the rear entrance to the Civic Center. The home of the Fox Sisters and other structures that had been Underground Railroad stations were also destroyed in order to built the new Inner Loop highway. When progress pushes history aside, even with well-meaning efforts to benefit a community, educational programs and tourism suffer irreplaceable loss.

Columbus Day, 1968 was a proud day for Joseph "Papa Joe" Fortino, whose dream of a bust of Christopher Columbus in the new Hall of Justice came true. In this photograph, Sheriff Skinner, Gordon Howe, and New York State Sen. Thomas Laverne congratulate him. "Papa Joe's" tribute to the Italian explorer launched several other movements to honor ethnic achievers.

The city's Polish community succeeded in obtaining a bust of the Revolutionary War hero Gen. Kosciusko at the Hall of Justice in 1970. Dr. Kusieliwicz, Fr. A. Stec, Gordon Howe, Vincent Parks, Nicholas Santoro, William Brodie, and Leonard Tomczak attended its dedication. With aid from the Susan B. Anthony Memorial, county historian Shirley Cox Husted succeeded in placing a bust of Susan B. Anthony and one of Rev. Thomas James, the city's first black pastor. Dennis Livadas spearheaded a drive to add a bust of Solon, the great lawgiver, through financial contributions from the Greek community.

With their thoughts on the skies, Francis H. Carroll, Ralph Schreiber, Reginald Sutherland, Claude Friday, Carl R. Bausch, Gordon Howe, and Clarence Smith are scanning a 1948 report on plans for a new Rochester-Monroe County airport. Times were changing, and the community had to change with them. The result of airport expansions spearheaded by the Honorable Gordon Howe and the Honorable Lucien Morin ultimately gave the community the Rochester International Airport, directed for many years by Sam Cooper.

Air Force One touched down at the new airport in 1970, bringing Pres. Richard M. Nixon and First Lady Patricia Nixon for a short visit. Legilator Henry Williams, Sen. Jacob Javitts, Rep. Charles Goodell, Rep. Barber Conable, Mayor Steven May, Gordon Howe, and Carl Hallauer were among the group welcoming them. A huge American flag hanging from the front of the county office building through arrangements by Fred "Bud" Herman drew the President's attention during a parade down Main Street. Before leaving, he shook hands with workmen building the city's new federal building, named in honor of Ambassador Kenneth B. Keating.

Gloves and shoestrings were offered for sale by E.L. Cory, an innovative disabled gentleman who made his own moveable store. Hucksters of vegetables and peddlers of merchandise of all kinds were once common. The gasoline shortages of WWII curtailed most of the "on the road" selling; door-to-door rag collectors and scissors and knife sharpeners disappeared, but street vendors will probably always be with us.

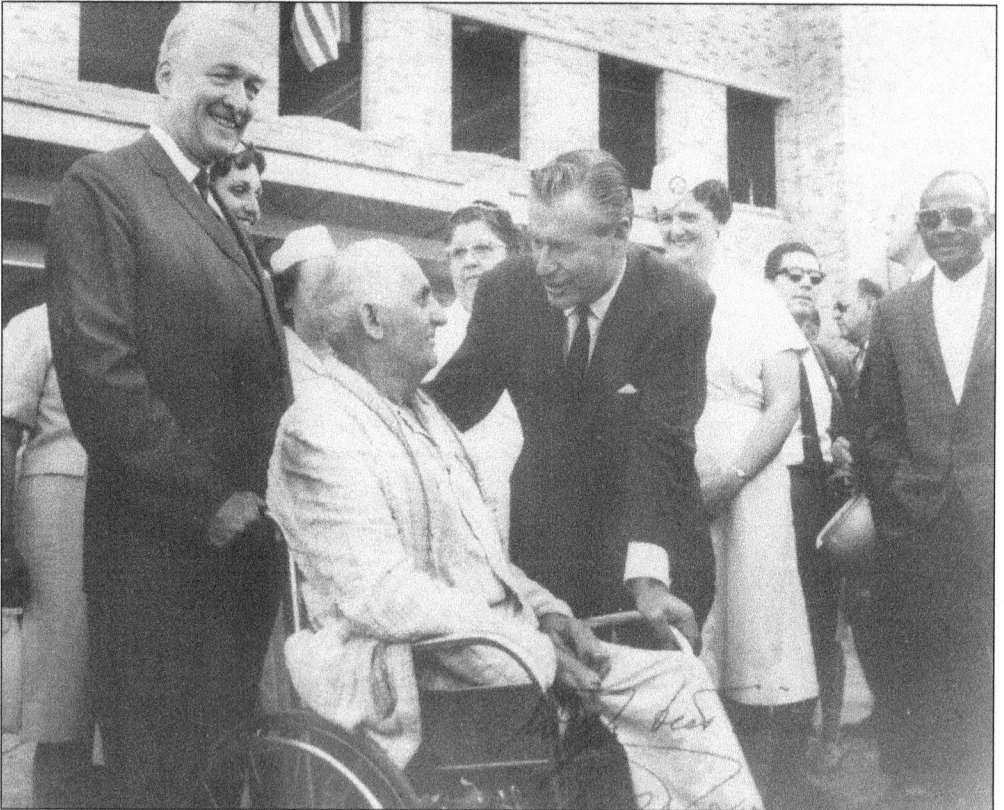

Governor Rockefeller expresses good wishes at ceremonies at the new social services facility under construction on Westfall Road. The old county hospital next-door had such lavish architecture that it became known as "the Poor Man's Palace," a surprising contrast to the modern brick skyscraper built during Howe's administration. Howe considered the signing of a contract allowing the University of Rochester doctors to care for indigent patients to be the greatest achievement of his career, inasmuch as it enabled the poorest of the poor to receive the best health care available.

The canal's vast waters east of the city near Culver Road have been mostly filled in. Lake Riley, a small remnant of the wide waters, is now part of Cobb's Hill Park. This view appeared on a 1910 postcard sent to the *Democrat and Chronicle* requesting cancellation of an advertisement reading, "Help Wanted, Female." Classifying jobs as suitable only for a certain sex was then customary.

Pinnacle Hill appears on this c. 1910 postcard showing the view from Cobb's Hill of the only mountain range in Monroe County. The Pinnacle Hills were shaped by an ancient Canadian glacier that once covered most of New York State, creating the hilly topography of Highland Park and Mount Hope Cemetery. In the Pinnacle Hill Catholic Cemetery on top of the hill, the revered hero Col. Patrick O'Rourke was buried. His unit's brave charge at Gettysburg stopped the advance of the South, turning the tide of the Civil War.

This attractive postcard view, looking west from Cobb's Hill, shows an early-20th-century neighborhood with a city skyline in the distance

As the city expanded, many typical city homes like these were built between 1910 and 1925. These Culver Road buildings were demolished in 1959 in order to allow construction of East High School. American Four Square homes like these, often expanded into rectangular apartment houses for city dwellers, usually featured a fine front porch where families could sit and greet passersby or wave to passing carriages during those slower paced, halcyon days before automobiles replaced horses.

After WWII, when building supplies again became available following a wartime lull in home building due to war shortages, many city residents had moved to the suburbs surrounding the city. A Field Street development near Clinton Avenue South in 1980 is typical of renewal projects that suddenly became popular when high gasoline prices forced families to move back to the city to avoid expensive commuting. Early-20th-century apartments stand nearby.

Civic Republican leaders included County Manager Gordon Howe, Sen. Kenneth Keating, and Rep. Barber B. Conable Jr. Conable, featured on a *Time* magazine cover and described as "the finest brain on the hill," readily cooperated with city officials to earmark federal funds for the Model Cities program. Howe's successor, the Honorable Lucien Morin, helped craft a history-making agreement with Mayor Thomas Ryan, increasing the city's share of sales taxes in order to avert a threatened bankruptcy. Keating's Mendon ancestor, Timothy Barnard, was also a congressman. After losing his Senate seat to Robert F. Kennedy, Keating became an ambassador.

As the county faced its future and celebrated its sesquicentennial in 1971, photographer Ernest Amato recorded Mayor Stephen May and Kermit Hill's presentation of the 1971–1972 city budget. Concern for the redevelopment of Charlotte and protection of what Howe loved to call "the Golden Shores of Lake Ontario" now began to receive increasing attention. The need to protect shore areas along Irondequoit Bay resulted in its designation as a National Shoreline after a new bay bridge connected Webster and Irondequoit by the city limits.

Redevelopment along the river, with some projects still underway, has materially changed this area along South Avenue once covered by railroad freight yards. Bridges, roads, and business improvements have brought many changes to the area.

Six

BY BEAUTIFUL WATERS

A wheelbarrow race was just one of many special activities held in city parks during the depression years. TERA funds for just one year provided a $76,000 payroll, with costs to the city of only $14,000. That year, practically every building in the city parks was repaired and painted. Several thousand picnic tables and benches were built or repaired in the repair shop at the old county home. Ping-pong tables and lifeboats were built. The hobby horses at Ontario Beach Park were revarnished and striped, and the carousel's tower was removed. An addition was made to the merry-go-round at Genesee Valley Park to provide shelter inside in case of inclement weather.

Swan boat rides on Trout Lake were once a popular Seneca Park attraction. Expansion of the zoo into this area is now planned. It would materially change the design developed by Frederick Law Olmsted, whose plan for several local parks as well as Central Park in New York City, attempted to preserve naturally landscaped areas in sharp contrast to built-up cityscapes.

The name of this black bear has not survived, but Oscar, a white polar bear was a very popular attraction at the Seneca Park Zoo. His picture appeared on boxes of popcorn sold at the zoo, as did a likeness of Jimmy the chimp. Penny and Nickels were Oscar's successors. Sally the elephant was also beloved, but in the 1980s controversy frequently surfaced over the need to provide much larger quarters for the elephants and other animals.

116

Irondequoit Bay was the destination of these fashionably dressed ladies, a trip possible about a century ago via a ride on the old Bay Rail Road. Visitors traveled to Irondequoit attractions, such as the Sea Breeze amusement park and "tony" restaurants at Newport, Point Pleasant, and other locations near Irondequoit Bay.

Forest Cottage had a trade card featuring the beautiful side-wheeler *Camille Forest* and a variety of treats for visitors to Sea Breeze in Irondequoit. The "cottage" was actually a large restaurant and hotel.

FOREST COTTAGE,

AT THE SEA-BREEZE,

Over the Bridge, on the left-hand side, as you leave the Depot, where you will find the very best of

LIQUORS AND CIGARS,

Also, **Cold Lunch** *of all descriptions.*

The *Harbor Belle* is seen at the Newport pier just north of the new bridge in 1993, when the little "belle" was getting old. The ship was a present-day tour boat reminiscent of the many steamboats, side-wheelers, and launches that have skimmed across the bay's deep waters. Private boats and canoes have explored the glorious scenery of the bay, and people have hunted and fished by it from time immemorial. Newport House, once the site of Hilfiker's lumbermill, has been re-created following a disastrous fire. A small marina is located there.

At the University of Rochester, beside the Genesee, the annual regatta is a popular event. Strong Memorial Hospital, the University's teaching hospital, continually expands its unique research facilities and provides excellent health care for the community. Also important to the community is the research done at the Rochester Institute of Technology. Since 75 internet-related local firms now employ thousands, cooperative telecommunications programs are underway with RIT as Rochester continues its historic role as a hub of expertise, discovery, and entrepreneurship.

The Lake Avenue Trolley began taking passengers north along the river to Charlotte and the lake shore in 1889. Their open-air horse-drawn trolleys offered picturesque rides to the Kodak Park area, to Holy Sepulchre Cemetery across from majestic St. Bernard's Seminary, or one could ride all the way to the beach. Because of a large Italian population, nuns and other riders could sometimes be overheard speaking Italian.

St. Bernard's Seminary was where generations of Roman Catholic priests were trained until its enrollment declined. The grounds where the priests once walked their outdoor Stations of the Cross have become part of Holy Sepulchre Cemetery. Adaptive uses have been found for the magnificent stone building complex that graces the riverbank near Charlotte.

Veteran's Memorial Bridge, a handsome span crossing the Genesee River near Kodak Park, was a very important project linking both sides of the river. The bridge made it possible for Irondequoit residents and city dwellers to find employment at Kodak Park, on the site of a former nursery. Hanford's Landing Road passes through the park and descends to the river by the cemetery, where some of the city's first pioneers lie buried. A prehistoric palisaded Native American village was once located here. Across the river from the landing on another Native American site are Seneca Park and its zoo, just off St. Paul Boulevard. The much detested traffic circle was later removed and replaced by housing. Many Kodak workers bought houses in Irondequoit or the city because this bridge made Kodak accessible.

The Wagg's Corners Store dominated Ridge Road at the Lake Avenue intersection across from Kodak Park. The store was built in 1902.

In 1915, this new "jitney" carried a small number of passengers along West Avenue for a modest 5¢ fare. The little jitney mini-busses became very popular. A jitney driven by Harvey Trabold ran out Ridge Road to Wagg's Corners and beyond, taking passengers to the Eastman Kodak area. His employer, the Ridge Road Transit Company, chartered in 1905, used chain-driven Knox busses.

The Charlotte Swing Bridge, built for the railroad in 1905, turned sideways in the river to open the way for the Ontario Coal and Car Ferry to pass by. Dredging sand and gravel to help clear the passage is underway by a turning basin. An old paint factory lies across the river in Irondequoit. Charlotte's railroad car yard is in the foreground. Because Rochester is the closest Great Lakes harbor to Pennsylvania's coal fields, trainloads of coal were frequently waiting to be shipped to Canada.

A harbor view is featured on this postcard view looking toward Charlotte from the Coast Guard station across the river. Riverside marinas offer pleasure boaters an entry to the river and lake. The flags of Ontario Beach Park are seen in the distance.

This port of Rochester scene was captured by Harry McCarty's camera. It offers a view of the good ship *Constance Bowater*. Occasional tours of visiting vessels are given, but the greatest modern attraction at Charlotte was the visit of tall-masted sailing ships during America's 1976 bicentennial, and a spectacular fireworks show accompanied with a concert by Rochester Philharmonic's talented musicians.

A trolley is making the turn at Lake Avenue near Kodak Park. One of the lures offered to promote the annexation of the Lake Avenue corridor to Charlotte in 1915 was the perk of a 5¢ ride to Ontario Beach Park. Known as "the Coney Island of the West," this summertime haven provided a bathing beach, amusement rides, boating, fishing, restaurants, beer gardens, a bathhouse, and a wooden boardwalk for lakeside strolls.

The blast furnace operated by the Rochester Iron Manufacturing Company at Charlotte provided pig iron for Rochester's foundries from 1869 until 1927. The company was the largest taxpayer in the village—one reason for a drive for annexation, as was acquisition of the Kodak Park plant. George Eastman promoted the annexation in order to obtain city water service for his film factory. Free school districts were an added enticement: those owning property within them would not have to pay school taxes. It was a controversial move, and newspapers called the annexation "the rape of Charlotte." It is a cleaver pun because Charlotte was named for the young daughter of its early land agent, Robert Troup.

Ontario Beach Park, a mecca for both children and adults, still has its whirling Denzil carousel, customarily called a merry-go-round by local residents. Admission at the gate was only 10¢, but if you came by train, admission was free.

Long piers extending more than 2,000 feet into the lake were built by the government in 1829, 1834, and 1882 to draw sand away from the river. The piers soon brought in several hundred feet of sand, creating a new shoreline and bathing beach. The city has built a new boardwalk by the beach to help re-create memories of yesteryears. Others have been preserved in displays at the 1822 lighthouse standing on the original shoreline, south of the beach.

A crowd often gathered near the bandstand at the beach for shows and musical performances. Those not in swimming carried umbrellas for protection against dangerous sun rays. In those days before sunscreen, vinegar rubs would be used to prevent or to heal sunburn.

One of Gordon Howe's first political accomplishments in 1926 was to obtain passage of a law that prevented males from appearing bare-chested on public beaches. Swimming suits for females covered all of the torso and included black stockings, bathing slippers, and bathing hats. (Mitchell photograph.)

These city children look very happy in this playground picture taken on August 14, 1913.

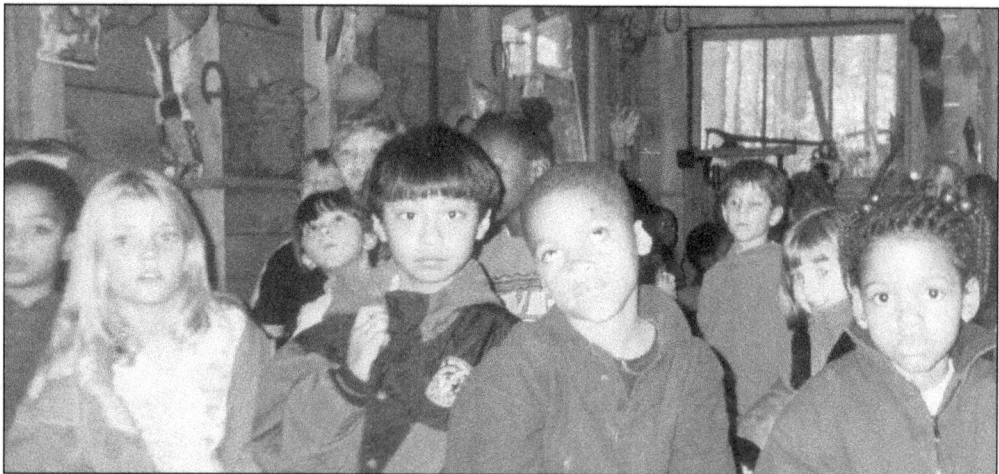

This group of children from a Rochester school is listening to the Native American storyteller during a 1998 field trip to McCracken Farms in the town of Sweden. This photograph demonstrates the ethnic mix of today's city schools. The Rochester these children know will change markedly in the future, as has the Rochester of the past. But while neighborhoods may change, fond memories of happy days and friendly people will most certainly live on.

Editor's note: For more detailed information on Rochester's many neighborhoods, see issues of *Rochester History*, published by the City Historian's Office, 115 South Avenue, Rochester, New York, 14604. Another volume in this series, *Rochester Volume II*, is also being contemplated.

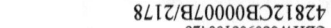